What Christians
Should Know About...

Escaping
From Debt

Keith Tondeur

Sovereign World

ISBN: 1 85240 235 0

SOVEREIGN WORLD LIMITED
P.O. Box 777, Tonbridge, Kent TN11 0ZS, England.

Typeset and printed in the UK by Sussex Litho Ltd, Chichester, West Sussex.

Contents

Introduction

This book has primarily been written for a British audience, but the principles it teaches are appropriate worldwide.

Two stories...

Michael was the director of a successful company. When the company hit hard times, he was made redundant and was called on to repay a debt of £30,000 for which he had given a personal guarantee. He got another job and started paying as much as he could – £150 a month. But his creditors carried on charging interest on the loan so that four years later the debt had actually risen to £44,000. On the edge of despair and ruin, Michael's marriage started to come apart at the seams.

Angela hadn't paid the rent for over three months – and she was hoping the landlord wouldn't notice. Her husband's low-paid job only just covered the food and clothing bills for them and their two young children. Angela lived in fear of a letter from the landlord and turned to valium to get her through each day. Then one day the letter she had been dreading finally arrived. She went to see the landlord. In total desperation she 'paid' the bill by sleeping with him. Angela hasn't been able to look in the mirror since.

Debt kills

Debt can have a crippling effect on the people trapped in it. It not only affects their bank balance, but the balance of their mind and their behaviour. Below are just a few of the ways in which debt can affect people:

Marriage breakdown. Debt can severely undermine relationships. A recent survey showed that over 70 per cent of couples who split up cited money problems as their main reason.

Child abuse. Financial pressure leads directly to stress at home. Parents can end up taking out their frustrations on their children, or might simply neglect them through worry about money.

Health problems. Shock, stress and depression over debt often lead to health problems, particularly in older people. Many people who lose their jobs or their standard of living, also end up losing their dignity and self-esteem.

Loss of friends. People who face severe money problems often withdraw from friends. If they go out, they cannot afford to pay their way and they cannot afford to entertain at home. Others find that friends desert them.

Despair and suicide. As businesses fail, houses are repossessed and years of debt repayment stretch ahead, it is not surprising that some people fall into despair, or simply give up.

Helplines to Contact

Credit Action Helpline:	0800 591084
National Debt Helpline:	0121 359 3562
Consumer Credit Counselling Service (CCCS):	0800 138 1111

The Aim of this Book

It is clear that the debt problem is not going to go away. This book is one attempt to do something about the problem. It does this in two ways. First, it shows that **people locked into debt are not powerless.** There are practical steps they can take to do something about their situation. And for those who are on the edge of debt, drifting into a crisis, this book shows how it can be avoided by taking action now.

Secondly, it shows that despite the real problems and hard decisions facing people in debt, **there is hope to be found.** This hope lies in the Christian good news, and in the love and support which can be given by Christians and churches.

What you can get out of this book

Why are you reading this? You might be doing so for a number of reasons:

You already have a debt problem. If you are already in debt, this book can offer you real help. Some sections may not apply to your specific situation but you will find plenty that do. Apart from offering friendly advice, the book also gives you some sample letters on which to base your own letters. Take time to read it through carefully – it could save you a lot of further heartache.

You have a potential debt problem. Debt might be on your horizon, but the storm hasn't hit you yet. Now is the time to take drastic action and this book can help you to do it.

You wish to help someone with a debt problem. There are almost certain to be people you know, or people in your church, who are in debt. This book will give you a greater insight into their situation and a greater ability to get alongside them with counselling and practical advice. Chapter 1 is a good place to start.

Opening up to Hope

This chapter looks at how debt affects people – how it plunges them into crisis and leads them into despair, guilt and loneliness. It also shows how our experience and the way we respond to it can be challenged and changed through the power of God.

You might be tempted to skip this chapter and go straight to chapter 2 which advises you on the practical steps you can take to improve your situation, but please don't. This chapter can offer you real hope, rather than a 'quick fix', to help you and your family. It can help you to start to face up to your situation, talk to those who are closest to you, and begin to regain some of your dignity.

Hitting the panic button

When debt strikes your entire world can be turned upside down. And when that happens it's the most normal thing in the world to hit the panic button.

You might have been made redundant. You might have received a court summons because of unpaid bills. You might have defaulted on your mortgage payment for the first time ever – or for the sixth month in a row. Your landlord might have started phoning you late at night to demand your overdue rent. Your gas might be disconnected, your TV or washing machine repossessed.

Any of these situations might be yours. In this no-man's land, most people are totally unprepared for what is happening and are completely unsure about what they should do next.

Debt is a stigma. It frequently leads to shame, guilt and loneliness. Because of the pressure it brings, debt can force perfectly normal people to do very unusual things. One well-respected businessman committed suicide the day before his house was due to be repossessed. This came as a terrible shock to his wife – he had not told her a thing about their money problems.

Panic leads to at least three patterns of behaviour which in turn add to the problem...

Closing your heart. Redundancy and sudden debt makes you feel small. One man who suddenly lost his job after years with the same company said, 'You feel like you've been kicked in the stomach'. Shock usually leads to a sense of despair. You close your heart to hope and feel that you have been stripped of all dignity.

Closing your eyes. Others try to avoid despair by pretending that it's not really happening. In a terrifying situation such as debt, closing your eyes can seem like the best option – but it isn't. Some people carry on spending, or even binge. Others refuse to look all their debts in the face to see what their true situation is like.

Closing down. Many people caught in a crisis of debt cannot face those who are closest to them. Their partners, children, family and friends are left in the dark about what is going on. At the time when they most need the help and support of others, they simply close down.

If any of these descriptions apply to you, then please read on. These three destructive patterns of behaviour can be changed for something better...

Opening your heart

If you are in despair because of your situation you can take some comfort (however small) from the fact that you are facing reality. Many people try to pretend that everything is all right and try to put away their natural feelings of worry and fear.

You may have a number of different feelings about yourself, your creditors and your situation. You might feel frightened, insecure, angry, badly treated, powerless, lost, ashamed, lonely, hopeless or resigned. You have hit really hard times. All these feelings show that you are trying to come to terms with what has happened. You wouldn't be human if you didn't experience some, or all, of these feelings.

What can you do with feelings like these?

Try not to squash them. Take your feelings seriously because they are registering that you have suffered a major blow. This is how God made you – a living, feeling person.

Try to talk about how you feel. If you keep your feelings to yourself you could end up feeling very isolated and misunderstood. Knowing that others understand how you feel can be a great relief.

Try telling God how you feel. God already understands your feelings but turning to Him in prayer lets you express yourself to God and draw comfort and strength from Him. As the Bible says: *'Cast all your anxiety on him, because he cares for you'* (1 Peter 5:7). Don't be afraid to get angry with God or express your darkest feelings to Him.

There is no quick and easy healing for the pain you feel. You have to face some hard facts. You may never again know the standard of living that you once enjoyed. This is very tough – particularly in our society, which places such a strong emphasis on the status of wealth.

The Bible gives no guarantees for an easy life but it does offer real hope. Whatever your circumstances, your true human worth and dignity lie with God. You may need a shift in your thinking to accept this. Perhaps you'll need to recognise that your security has always been built on a certain standard of living rather than on God Himself – the source of all security. Jesus once said: *'Do not store up for yourselves treasures on earth, where moth and rust destroy, and where thieves break in and steal. But store up for yourselves treasures in heaven... For where your treasure is, there your heart will be also'* (Matthew 6:19-21).

What does it mean to *'store up treasure in heaven'*? Jesus is talking about a hope on which we can start to rebuild our lives.

God made us and is with us. He understands our lives from beginning to end. Read and pray through Psalm 139. Here are some of the things it says: *'Where can I go from your Spirit? Where can I flee from your presence? If I go up to the heavens, you are there; if I make my bed in the depths, you are there...'* (Psalm 139:7-8). God understands our thoughts and feelings and

11

knows the true meaning of our lives.

God loves us and has plans for us. Even in hard times, God still loves us. It can be hard to believe that God cares about what is happening to us when everything around seems to be collapsing. At one of their all-time low points God's people in the Bible were promised: *'"I know the plans I have for you," declares the Lord, "plans to prosper you and not to harm you, plans to give you hope and a future"'* (Jeremiah 29:11).

God hears our cries for help. No matter how weak or powerless we feel in the face of debt God hears us and sends us help. This **doesn't** mean that if we can only pray harder our debts will dissolve. God's help might come in many different ways: a new friendship, inner encouragement, a change in circumstances, overcoming fear. *'I sought the Lord and he answered me; he delivered me from all my fears'* (Psalm 34:4).

However your debt crisis came about, you can come to see it as a test of your character and your faith in God. This is easy to put down in words, and much harder to live through – but it comes with a promise from the Bible: *'Blessed are they who persevere under trial, because when they have stood the test, they will receive the crown of life that God has promised to those who love him'* (James 1:12).

If you are able to seize the new hope that God offers you, you will be in a much stronger position to start tackling your debt problems. New hope and new life do not come easily. You might need to repent and seek God's forgiveness. Or you might need to throw yourself on Him because you have been hurt by the injustice of others. Whatever your need, as you read the Bible, take time to pray, and talk and pray with others; your life can be renewed from the inside.

Opening your eyes

You might think that if being real about your situation will lead you into despair then it's better to pretend. Better to carry on as if your debt crisis was simply not happening at all. Spend your way out of a crisis.

Or perhaps you find that your life has simply switched on to autopilot. You no longer have the desire or strength to do something about your situation. Letters go unanswered, final demands pile up, phone calls are put off and you find it hard to talk about it at all.

If this is how you are at the moment then this section is here to flash a red warning light at you: you are in danger! If you fail to recognise what is happening and continue to ignore the warning signs you will very quickly hit disaster. At this point in your life pretending and doing nothing are the very last things that can help you.

There are several things you can do to open your eyes to where you are now.

Be real. Your first need is to face up to your situation, even though it is painful to do so. One verse in the Bible says: *'Wake up! Strengthen what remains and is about to die...'* (Revelation 3:2). You might find that the best way to wake up is to confide in a friend, a church leader or counsellor. Tell them about how you feel, and why you find it difficult to face the facts. Simply talking about it will give you a better understanding of yourself and the other person may be able to offer real help and support.

Act responsibly. Your mortgage, rent, tax and any other money worries are your responsibility (or a responsibility shared with your partner). You need to take up your God-given responsibility to safeguard yourself and your family and to honour your debts to the best of your ability.

● If your finances are not yet in crisis you should look at ways of cutting back on your spending and living within your means.

● If you are already in financial trouble you can make a first step by realising that you are not powerless. You have legal rights and courses of action that can make a real difference to your situation.

Take action. If you do nothing your crisis will grow worse. You need to take action now – and this book will help you do just that.

Sooner or later the reality of your situation will come home to you. It may even be forced upon you. It is better – far better – to come to terms with it now while there are still plenty of things you can do about it.

Opening up

Stephen was running into heavy debt but he couldn't talk about it with his family. He simply froze when his wife or teenage children mentioned the problems they knew existed. Susan, his daughter, was scared she would have to leave her fee-paying school and things reached crisis point when she ran away and was missing for three weeks.

Closing down communication is something that happens especially (though not exclusively) to men. Men who fall into debt often feel guilt, failure and shame very deeply indeed. This can result in withdrawal from family and friends, or in outbursts of disturbed behaviour. This is exactly how Stephen felt: 'I've got myself into this problem and I've got to get out of it by myself.'

The trouble is situations like this cannot be tackled alone. You need all the advice, discussion, love and support that you can get from those around you. Perhaps the best way to start is to ask what it is that stops you from talking with others. There could be several reasons.

Barriers to opening up

- Fear of any financial mistakes coming to light.
- Fear of someone saying, 'I told you so.'
- Not wanting to face the anger of your partner.
- The humiliation of losing face with family and friends.
- Fear of admitting there is a problem when everything appears OK.
- Dreading the thought of saying 'sorry.'
- Fear that others will reject you.

These are strong fears. You cannot dismiss them lighlty. If you have fears like these you should take time to think about them and, if possible, bring them to God in prayer. Ask Him to deliver you from the power of your fears. Opening up to God may well be the best way to start opening up to others.

Then you need to take the plunge and start talking. Some of your fears may come to pass while others simply vanish. You may find that some friends will find it hard to stay in touch with you – but those who are closest to you should be able to give you great support.

Making contact with your partner. Above all, make sure that you talk honestly with your partner. Let him or her know the full situation. Share how you feel about it and listen carefully to his or her feelings as well. If you have concealed information for a long time you will probably be on the receiving end of shock and a lot of anger.

You should take time to allow your bad news to sink in and not try to cover up your partner's hurt feelings. In this case, you will also need to be reconciled and you might not be able to do this on your own. If your partner's anger and resentment persist you could suggest talking together with a third party such as one of your church leaders.

On your own? If you find yourself on your own without family or friends who can help you, local Christians may be able to offer real support. If you don't belong to a church try getting in touch with one locally. Many churches today have small groups that meet in the home to talk, pray and read the Bible together. This could be just what you need.

You may also find in the church fellowship, someone experienced in financial matters who would be willing to help and advise in your particular situation.

The Christian community at its best is a place where you can find acceptance and practical help. Paul the apostle wrote about what such communities can mean: *'Love must be sincere. Hate what is evil; cling to what is good. Be devoted to one another in brotherly love. Honour one another above yourselves ... Be joyful in hope, patient in affliction, faithful in prayer. Share with God's people who are in need. Practise hospitality'* (Romans 12:9-10, 13).

Steps to Take

Step 1. Contact all creditors

Creditors cannot help you unless they are aware of your difficulties and circumstances. You may also need to ask them for full details of the amount owing, actual arrears, penalty charges etc. The following is a typical letter:

Your address

Date

Dear Sirs

Account/Agreement Number

I am currently experiencing financial difficulties due to .... and I am therefore unable to maintain the full payment on my account. I am trying to resolve my situation and will send you a financial statement as soon as possible with the best payment offer I can manage.

Please let me have the following information so that I can draw up a schedule of all my debts and make appropriate offers to my creditors:

Type of agreement (secured/unsecured)

Balance owing

Terms of repayment and interest/penalties accruing

Arrears

I will write to you again as soon as I have received replies from all my creditors.

Yours faithfully

When all the replies have been received draw up a schedule of your debts and divide them between **Priority** and **Secondary** creditors (see Step 2). It is essential at this stage to mark any debts where court orders (County Court Judgments or CCJs) have been made or summons received and seek specialist help as these debts need **immediate** attention.

Keep copies of all correspondence both sent and received. If any agreements are subsequently made by telephone get the name of the person you spoke to and ensure that the agreement is confirmed in writing.

It is important to check that you are actually responsible for all your debts. A husband and wife are not responsible for each other's debts unless they have **both** signed the agreement (except for Council Tax), and you cannot inherit a dead person's debts.

You should also check the amount being claimed to ensure all the payments you have made have been deducted, and challenge any excessive interest or penalty charges.

Step 2. Decide Priorities

Some debts carry more severe penalties than others and this means that they must be dealt with first. Priority treatment is not determined by the size of the debt, the period or amount of arrears or the threats being made, but by the actual legal remedy the creditor has against you for recovery. A **Priority** debt is usually defined as one where non-payment can result in you:

- being imprisoned
- losing your home
- losing essential goods or services.

Opposite is a list of priority debts and the legal consequences of non-payment:

Type of debt	Final sanctions for non-payment
Mortgage/secured loan	Loss of house
Rent	Eviction
Gas/electricity/water	Disconnection
Council tax	Taken from wages/benefits; bailiffs; imprisonment
CSA/maintenance orders	Taken from wages/benefits; imprisonment
Magistrates fines	Bailiffs; imprisonment
Inland Revenue and VAT	Bailiffs; bankruptcy, imprisonment

Prioirity creditors must be dealt with before any offers or payments are made on **Secondary** debts. **Secondary** debts are all those which do not carry the above sanctions. For example:

Type of debt	Final sanction for non-payment
Credit/store cards	County Court Judgment
Personal loan (unsecured)	County Court Judgment
Bank loan/overdraft	County Court Judgment
Hire purchase*	Loss of goods
Credit sale	County Court Judgment
Catalogue†	County Court Judgment
Pawnbroker	Keep pledge
Loan shark‡	Not legally enforceable unless licensed
Loan from family/friends‡	County Court Judgment

*If the threatened goods are an essential requirement, for example a washing machine or car needed for work, such a debt must be treated as priority, but if you have paid less than one third of the total owed under the hire purchase agreement the creditor can repossess the goods without a court order.

†Catalogue debts may be difficult to enforce as it is not always standard practice to complete a formal credit agreement, and creditors should be asked to produce a copy of this if proceedings

are threatened. Some catalogue companies have a payment protection plan for circumstances such as unemployment and sickness which may cover your debt to them.

‡Individual circumstances may suggest some other debts be treated as priority, although not legally enforceable, e.g. money owed to family, friends or loan sharks.

Before you make offers of payment to any creditors you will need to prepare a financial statement – see Step 3 that follows.

Step 3. Prepare a Financial Statement

It is essential that you now prepare a statement of your actual current financial position. A specimen is shown on the following page and can be adapted to suit your particular situation. Your statement must include **all** income received from whatever source and **all** money going out and to where.

When completing this form use either weekly or monthly figures, but don't mix them and mark clearly on the statement which basis you have used.

To change weekly figures to monthly, multiply by 52 and then divide by 12.

To change monthly figures to weekly multiply by 12 and then divide by 52.

Annual payments such as TV licence, road tax, insurance premiums etc. should be divided by 12 to give the monthly amount or by 52 for the weekly figure.

Also allow for irregular, and often unexpected, expenditure such as car and house maintenance, repairs and replacements.

The example financial statement has not included your giving as a Christian, but this should continue to be a priority as far as is possible.

It is important to take everything into account, but don't include payments for arrears or secondary creditors at this stage because you need to know the total money you have available (if any) to make offers to them.

Before finalising your statement you must review your **income** to see if it can be increased in any way (see Step 4) and consider your **expenditure** to ascertain if any savings can be made (see Step 5).

Your financial statement will need to be constantly revised to reflect changes in your income and expenditure and to incorporate subsequent agreements for payments to be made to your creditors.

FINANCIAL STATEMENT			
DATE PREPARED			
NAME			
ADDRESS			
No. of adults in household		No. of children in household	
INCOME weekly/monthly			
	YOU	PARTNER	**TOTAL**
WAGES			
PART-TIME JOB			
CHILD BENEFIT			
JOB SEEKERS ALLOWANCE			
DISABILITY & SICKNESS BENEFIT			
PENSION			
CHILD MAINTENANCE PAID TO YOU			
RENT OR MONEY FROM LODGERS			
OTHER			
OTHER			
TOTAL HOUSEHOLD INCOME			

EXPENDITURE weekly/monthly	
PRIORITIES	**Amount spent**
Giving	
Mortgage/Rent/Board	
2nd Mortgage/Secured Loan	
Endowment Policy	
Child Maintenance Paid by You	
Council tax	
Water Charges	
Electricity	
Gas	
Service Charges/Ground Rent	
Court Fines/County Court Judgments	
Vehicle Finance/Hire Purchase	
Television Licence	
Self Employed	
Income Tax	
National Insurance	
VAT	
LIVING COSTS	
Food and Housekeeping	
School Meals/Meals at Work	
Clothing/Footwear	
Vehicle Running Costs (Tax,Insurance, etc)	
Petrol/Diesel	
Fares (Bus, Train, etc)	
Telephone	
Rentals (TV, Video, etc)	
Prescriptions/Dentist/Optician	
Childminder/Nursery	
School Costs	
Cigarettes/Alcohol	
Life Insurance/Pension/Investments	
Building/Contents Insurance	
Other	
TOTAL HOUSEHOLD COSTS (1)	
TOTAL HOUSEHOLD INCOME (2)	
TOTAL LEFT AFTER TAKING (1) FROM (2)	

Step 4. Income Maximisation

Be sure that you have included everything, and then consider if you can obtain any additional income. Possibilities might be:

- **Job Seekers Allowance** – if you are unemployed or have been made redundant.
- **Family Credit** – if you are working but on a low income.
- **Income Support** – is available to people on low incomes and who meet certain criteria relating to work, sickness, age, savings etc. Check with your local Benefits Agency whether you are entitled to this.
- **Incapacity or disablement benefits,** including mobility or attendance allowance.
- **Income Tax** – check your tax code, particularly if your circumstances have changed, as you may be entitled to a rebate.
- **Maintenance** – are you entitled to this? Contact the Child Support Agency.
- **Housing Benefit** and **Council Tax relief** – your local council can advise on eligibility for these.
- What about part-time work or taking in a lodger?
- Can grown-up children or non-dependants contribute towards the household expenses?

Seek help from the Benefits Agency, your local council, Inland Revenue or one of the helplines listed in the introduction if you are not sure of your entitlement.

Income maximisation is a very important part of the debt resolution process and creditors will want to be reassured that you have considered all the options.

Step 5. Expenditure Review

It is important to include all household expenditure and financial commitments in your statement, whether regular or irregular. Variable items such as fuel bills should be averaged out over the year and the use of budget plans, stamps or tokens may assist with this.

Creditors may challenge amounts spent on food, fuel, clothing, travel etc., so is there any way that you can reduce these to realistic levels in relation to the size and circumstances of your family? The cost of running a car may need to be justified against using public transport. For example, is it essential to travel by car to work, school or on shopping trips because other means of transport are not available? Leisure and holiday costs may also be challenged by creditors, along with expenditure on cigarettes, alcohol, the lottery and pets etc.

Once again check your expenditure carefully to be sure that everything is included and all reasonable savings have been made. Try and make your expenses less than your income, otherwise your debts will continue to grow. However, do be realistic, as you may have to live on this budget for several years, so concentrate on reducing non-essentials rather than basics such as food and heating.

On completion of your income and expenditure review you can now finalise your financial statement before sending it to your creditors as part of your negotiations with them (see Steps 6 and 7).

Step 6. Negotiate with Priority Creditors

On completion of your financial statement deduct your total expenditure from your total income to see what money (if any) you have towards clearing your debts.

You will first need to negotiate with your priority creditors (see Step 2 for definition) and this should be done quickly to prevent implementation of their sanctions. Even if legal proceedings for recovery have commenced it is never too late to make an offer and seek a voluntary agreement.

List all your priority debts and send this schedule, along with your financial statement, to each priority creditor. This letter should detail the reasons for your financial difficulties and include a reasonable offer for payment of arrears, provided there is surplus money available. A suggested letter is as follows:

Your address

Date

Dear Sirs

Account/Agreement Number

I am experiencing financial difficulties because
.... I enclose a financial
statement detailing my current situation together with a
schedule of all my priority creditors.

You will appreciate that it is necessary for me to make an
offer to each of these creditors, therefore I am able to pay
you £................. per week/month. If you will confirm
your agreement in writing I will commence payments
immediately. Please also advise me of the method and due
date for such payments.

Yours faithfully

When negotiating with your creditors:

- You should not offer all your available income to one creditor.
- Start your negotiations with the debt nearest to its final sanction.
- Don't feel obliged/feel pressurised to pay more than you can afford, as it is important to sustain the payments once agreed.
- Even if creditors don't agree to your initial offer, start paying as it will begin to reduce your arrears and may persuade them to change their minds if they see that you are serious in your intentions.
- Ensure that you get a receipt for all payments made and any verbal agreements must be confirmed in writing.

As **payment is agreed with each creditor you should include this in your financial statement** so that other creditors can see your current situation and you can adjust to living within your new budget.

If you have no surplus income for priority creditors after re-assessing your budget you must still contact them and support your position with your financial statement. You should remember that some creditors have the legal right to make direct deductions from wages or income support via the Benefits Agency.

For 'fuel debts', pre-payment meters allow the arrears to be collected over a period of time and are a way of avoiding disconnection.

For **mortgages and secured loans** the following options should be explored:

- Never abandon your property or hand the keys back to the lender.
- Always contact your mortgage lender at the first sign of a problem and continue to keep them informed of any changes in your circumstances.
- Inquire about switching to 'interest only' or other reduced payments for a limited period of time.
- Capitalise the arrears.
- If your financial situation is improving, seek to repay the arrears over an agreed period of time.
- Consider re-mortgaging on a different basis, e.g. transferring from an endowment to a repayment mortgage, but be careful to check and compare terms and conditions, initial and longer-term interest rates, early redemption penalties, administration charges etc. It would be good to seek independent advice in this area.
- Voluntary sale of the home will usually produce a higher price than forced sale after repossession, but consideration must first be given to alternative accommodation as the local authority may decide that you have intentionally made yourself homeless. Such a sale may not always produce sufficient equity to clear the outstanding mortgage/loan and

you may still be legally liable for the balance, even if the lender agreed to the sale.

Step 7. Negotiate with Secondary Creditors

After agreeing offers of repayment for all your priority debts, your financial statement should be updated to see if you have any disposable income to pay your non-priority debts (see Step 2 for definition). The fairest way to divide this amount (if any) amongst the secondary creditors is in proportion to the total amount they are owed. List these remaining debts on a summary sheet (see example below) and add up the total of the secondary debts. The total available disposable income is then apportioned to these creditors by the following method:

$$\frac{\text{Individual debt}}{\text{Total debts}} \quad x \quad \text{Disposable income} \quad = \quad \text{Offer}$$

The example given below assumes you have £100.00 per month available for all secondary creditors:

SCHEDULE OF SECONDARY CREDITORS

Name:

Date:

CREDITOR	AMOUNT OWED	OFFER (per month)
	£	£
ABC Catalogue	2,000.00	20.00
Northern Loans	3,000.00	30.00
Right Car Finance	1,000.00	10.00
Flexible Credit Card	4,000.00	40.00
TOTAL	10,000.00	100.00

Using the above formula the calculation for the Flexible Credit Card would be :

$$\frac{£4{,}000.00}{£10{,}000.00} \quad x \quad £100.00 \quad = \quad £40.00$$

You may find it helpful to use a calculator to complete this schedule.

Using the figures you have calculated you can make an offer to each secondary creditor. A typical letter is shown below and this should be supported by a copy of the debt schedule and your financial statement.

> Your address
>
> Date
>
> Dear Sirs
>
> Account/Agreement Number
> You will be aware from my earlier letter that I am experiencing financial difficulties due to...................................
>
> I enclose a copy of my current financial statement which includes payment of arrears to my priority creditors. I also enclose a schedule of all my secondary debts from which you will see the available money has been apportioned on a pro rata basis.
>
> I ask that you will accept this offer of £............per month and stop interest or other charges accruing in order that the payments will begin to reduce the debt.
>
> Please confirm your acceptance in writing and advise me how the payments should be made.
>
> Thank you in anticipation.
>
> Yours faithfully

It is important that creditors can see that you have treated each of them fairly so don't be pressurised or threatened into increasing individual offers at the expense of other creditors. There is usually a reluctance to freeze interest and other charges but there is little point in paying if the outstanding balance continues to rise so try writing again as follows:

Your address
Date

Dear Sirs

Account/agreement number

Thank you for accepting my offer of repayment but I am disappointed that you have not agreed to freeze the interest on the account. As you will appreciate, if the interest is not stopped then the balance on the account will continue to rise and I will never be able to repay the debt. I would ask, therefore, that you reconsider your decision and advise me accordingly.

Yours faithfully

If your bank is a secondary creditor it may be necessary to open an account elsewhere if possible and redirect your wages so that you can have access to them. Direct debits will also need to be transferred as the bank may stop paying them.

Start payments as soon as they are agreed in writing with your creditors and remember that **keeping up regular payments is essential**, even if they are small.

If your circumstances deteriorate further and you cannot sustain payments then prepare a revised financial statement, re-calculate your offers in line with your current available disposable income and write to your creditors again explaining the change in your circumstances.

If a creditor will not accept your initial offer you can write to them as follows:

```
                                                    Your address
                                                    Date
Dear Sirs

Account/agreement number

Thank you for your letter dated.................................

I am sorry that you feel unable to accept my offer. The
majority (or all) of my other creditors have accepted and
payments to them have commenced. I cannot offer you more
as you will see from my financial statement that I have only
£.................. in total between all my creditors and it would be
unfair to favour your company at the expense of others who
have agreed to my offer.

Please reconsider your decision in the light of what the other
creditors have accepted.

Yours faithfully
```

Often creditors will agree to reduced payments for a limited
period of time, for example three to six months. If your
circumstances haven't improved by the end of this period then let
them know and continue existing payments. Otherwise prepare an
updated financial statement and re-calculate your offers as
explained above.

If you have **no disposable income for secondary creditors**
then write and inform them explaining your circumstances and
sending your financial statement to confirm your situation. Agree
to contact them again if your circumstances improve. In the
meantime ask them to freeze interest charges. You could ask them
to consider writing off the debt or accepting a reduced settlement,
although they are unlikely to do so in the early stages. You could
write as follows:

> Your address
>
> Date
>
> Dear Sirs
>
> Account/agreement number
>
> I am experiencing financial difficulties because.......................
> .... I enclose a copy of my financial
> statement from which you will see that after meeting essential
> expenditure there is no available income with which I can
> make you an offer.
>
> If my circumstances improve in the future I will contact you
> again but in the meantime will you freeze the interest charges
> and consider whether you will write off the debt?
>
> Yours faithfully

Court Proceedings

The aim of this booklet is to help you avoid court proceedings,
but what happens if negotiation fails and your creditors resort to
legal action? It is not a crime just to owe money and, with certain
exceptions (see Step 2), you can't go to jail if you are unable to
pay. Your case will normally be heard in the county court which is
not a criminal court. The court is not there to punish you but to
ensure fairness between the borrower and lender. So don't be
afraid of court action – it can often help solve your problem
because you do have some legal rights.

Always complete and return court documents within the
specified time so that the court is aware of your problems and
overall financial situation. They will be able to take these into
consideration when making an order.

Always attend court hearings to ensure that your case is
properly represented. The case will normally be heard in a private
room with officials who are used to dealing with these matters –
they are not there to serve the interests of the creditor alone.

It is helpful to be represented in court, but don't worry if you
cannot afford a solicitor, just contact your local Citizens Advice

Bureau who can arrange assistance or telephone one of the helplines mentioned in the introduction to this booklet.

If court action is taken against you:

- You will receive a Default Summons stating what your creditor claims from you.
- If you do owe the money, return the form of reply attached to the summons to the creditor saying how much you can pay. Complete the financial statement on the back of the summons and make sure you explain your circumstances fully.
- If you dispute some or all the debt, say why on the form provided.
- If the creditor accepts your offer they will tell the court and you will then get an order (a judgement – CCJ) from the court telling you to pay at the rate you offered.
- If the creditor refuses your offer the court decides how much you pay from the information you have provided. If they tell you to pay more than you have offered you can ask for a hearing to explain your situation in more detail. You have fourteen days to ask for this.
- Seek advice in dealing with court documents but don't ignore them otherwise a decision will be made without the court being aware of your actual circumstances and financial situation.
- Special considerations apply if the court hearing is for re-possession of or eviction from your home – seek immediate help as there are still things you can do at this stage.

Other aspects of **debt recovery procedures** that you may become involved with are:

Debt collection agencies
Rather than accept your offer of repayment the creditor may refer your account to a debt collector. Do not be pressured, bullied or threatened by them into paying more than you can afford. Stand

firm on your offer and refer to the financial statement sent to the creditor. Collectors have no legal right of entry to your home and cannot remove goods. Undue harassment should be reported to your local Trading Standards Department.

Bailiffs

If you fail to make the payments under a CCJ the court will grant a Warrant of Possession Order and bailiffs will act on behalf of the court to implement that order by removing certain goods to the value of the debt and costs. You do not have to let a bailiff into your home and they cannot break in (unless they have entered previously for that debt). They can legally enter through a door or window that you have left open. Only bailiffs recovering debts owed to the State (e.g. Income Tax and VAT) can force entry to your home. Even at this late stage it may be possible to negotiate satisfactory terms for payment with the bailiff. As an alternative the court can grant an Attachment of Earnings Order to deduct money directly from your wages.

Credit reference agencies

They keep records of some unpaid debts and a register of all county court judgements. Most companies will check with an agency before giving credit. You can obtain a copy of your record from the Agency and if it is wrong it can be corrected and when you pay off a CCJ you can have your record marked accordingly. Full details of these procedures are contained in a free booklet entitled 'No Credit' which you can get from your local Trading Standards Office.

Magistrates Court

Certain types of debt can be recovered through the Magistrates Court (e.g. council tax arrears and unpaid fines). The procedure will vary but once again you must respond to all court documents and immediately seek professional advice. The magistrates have the ultimate sanction of imprisonment for some debts, although this is only used as a last resort.

Administration Orders

If you have a number of small debts (maximum £5,000 in total) you can apply to the court for an Administration Order. This means that you pay the court one regular amount and they distribute it to the creditors on your behalf, although a small charge is made. A court judgement has to be entered against you before you can apply.

Bankruptcy/Individual Voluntary Arrangement (IVA)

Bankruptcy is a way of dealing with debts, enabling you eventually to make a fresh start and, at the same time, making sure your assets are shared out fairly amongst your creditors. However, you will lose your available assets and there are costs and restrictions on your future activities so the situation needs very careful consideration and you should seek professional advice before making a decision. Your creditors can also petition for a Bankruptcy Order and, if this is the case you need to seek help immediately.

An IVA is another way of resolving a debt problem. Certain criteria must be met and there are costs involved. You must also have some means of making an offer to creditors. Seek professional advice before embarking on this complex procedure.

Conclusions – the Future

The path to clearing your debts, or even avoiding them, may be quite short for some. On the other hand, you could be faced with several years of hardship before you are able to clear them. In either case you need to identify the cause of your problem. Most people fall into debt through no fault of their own. It is often as a result of redundancy or reduced working hours, illness or marriage breakdown. However, it may be that you found using credit cards was too easy or you were unable to resist offers of interest-free credit.

One of the key things to remember is that family pressures will arise. Not only will you have less money, but also your stress and anxiety levels are likely to increase. It is important to realise that this is perfectly natural and understandable so please don't be afraid to seek help and medical advice if necessary. If you have lost your job, try to keep yourself occupied. You might find it helpful to join a local support group if there is one in your area.

Below are a few practical suggestions for saving money and staying out of debt in the future:

- Only buy on a cash basis – if you can't afford something save up for it.
- When you go to buy something ask yourself whether you really **need** it or just **want** it. Try waiting for thirty days before you buy anything and if you decide you are going to buy it try and obtain one or two quotations to compare prices.
- When you go shopping prepare a list and keep to it.
- Keep you financial statement up to date and live within it.
- Look for ways to improve your income whilst trying to reduce your expenditure.
- Keep your own accounts and always check your bank statement.
- Budget for non-regular bills and expenses.
- Educate all members of your family in managing their own

finances – you could be preventing much heartache in future years.

● Start a regular savings plan – no matter how small the amount.

Remember – if debts start to build up again seek immediate help before things get too far out of hand.

Some Do's and Don'ts

☑ DO   be realistic – face up to your true situation and resolve to deal with it – using the help available to you.

☑ DO   get in touch with your creditors immediately to explain your difficulties.

☑ DO   give priority to those debts which may result in you losing your home, fuel supplies or your liberty.

☑ DO   remember that your creditors prefer small payments regularly rather than larger payments that you cannot sustain.

☑ DO   reply to creditors' letters and court summonses within the time period specified and let them have all the facts.

☑ DO   keep copies of all correspondence, financial statements, debt schedules etc.

☑ DO   attend and/or be represented at court hearings and take all relevant correspondence with you, including your current financial statement.

☑ DO   remember that ultimately your security should be in God **not** in money.

☑ DO   seek the prayer support of Christians to encourage you.

☒ DON'T   ignore the problem – it **won't** go away.

☒ DON'T give up trying to reach agreement with your creditors even if they are difficult and refuse your initial offers.

☒ DON'T be threatened or bullied into making promises that you cannot fulfil.

☒ DON'T borrow more money to pay off your debts, especially by taking on more credit or store cards.

☒ DON'T be afraid to ask for specialist advice – its **free** (see telephone numbers in the introduction to this booklet).

☒ DON'T try and struggle alone.

If you have enjoyed this book and would like to help us to send a copy of it and many other titles to needy pastors in the **Third World**, please write for further information or send your gift to:

Sovereign World Trust, P.O. Box 777, Tonbridge, Kent TN11 0ZS, United Kingdom

or to the **'Sovereign World'** distributor in your country.